ULTIMATE GUIDE

TO GETTING MORE TRAFFIC, LEADS AND SALES FOR YOUR LOCAL BUSINESS

TOPRANKEDVIDEO.COM
EXPERIENCE THE POWER OF VIDEO MARKETING

Are you **tired of paying for expensive pay-per-click advertising** and getting little in return? My name is Matthew May. I have **generated $100,000's is sales online** consistently using almost exclusively free or very low-cost advertising methods.

I have created the following ebook giving the local business owner a **guide on how to get started promoting their local business** online using the latest and most efficient methods.

If you are interested in some learning more about our local marketing packages or wish to have a personal consultation, please visit Toprankedvideo.com

Wishing you much success with your local business!

Matthew May
Toprankedvideo.com

1. Optimize Your Google My Business Page

If you have not done so already. The **first step** to getting more sales traffic and leads to your local business is setting up and optimizing your **Google My Business Page.**

This is the page you see at the **top of the search listings** whenever you search for a **local business**. See below:

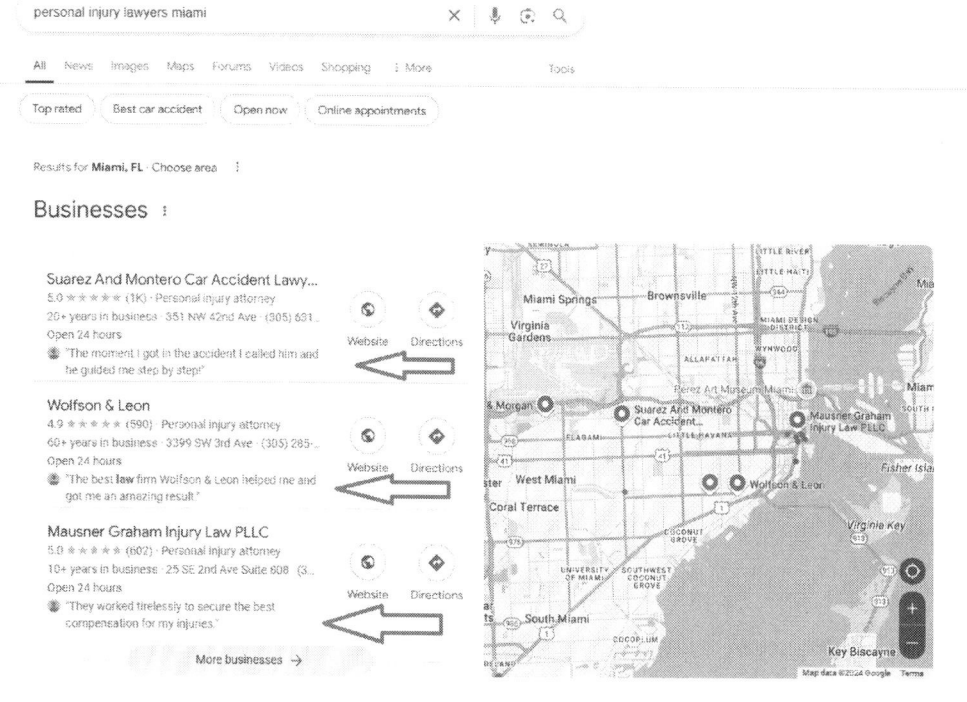

What Is Google My Business (GMB)?

Google My Business (GMB), now called **Google Business Profile**, is a **free tool** that helps businesses manage their online presence across Google, **including Search and Maps**. **Optimizing your profile** ensures **better visibility in local searches** and helps attract more customers.

Getting Started With Google My Business

1. **Create an Account**:
    - Go to <u>Google Business Profile</u>.
    - Sign in with your Google account.
    - Click "Manage Now" and follow the prompts to create your profile.
2. **Claim Your Business**:
    - Search for your business on Google.
    - If it exists, click "Claim this Business" and verify your ownership.
3. **Verify Your Business**
- Verification ensures that only authorized persons manage the profile. Verification

methods include:
- **Postcard by Mail**: Google sends a postcard with a verification code.
- **Phone or Email**: Instant verification for eligible businesses.
- **Bulk Verification**: Available for businesses with multiple locations.

4. Complete Your Business Profile

Fill out every section of your profile accurately and thoroughly.

1. **Business Name**:
   - Use the exact name of your business as it appears in the real world.
2. **Category and Attributes**:
   - Choose the most relevant primary category (e.g., "Italian Restaurant").
   - Add secondary categories and attributes like "Women-Led" or "Outdoor Seating."
3. **Address and Service Area**:
   - Enter your physical address (if applicable) and define your service area.
4. **Contact Information**:
   - Include a phone number and website URL.
   - Ensure consistency with information on your website and other directories.
5. **Business Hours**:
   - Update regular and holiday hours.
6. **Business Description**:
   - Write a compelling 750-character description.
   - Focus on what makes your business unique and include local keywords.
7. **Photos and Videos**:
   - Add high-quality images and videos of your storefront, products, and services.
   - Types of photos to include:
     - **Logo**: For branding.
     - **Cover Photo**: Main image customers see.
     - **Interior/Exterior**: Showcase your premises.
     - **Team and Product Photos**: Build trust.

5. Optimize for Local SEO

1. **Include Keywords**:
   - Use relevant local keywords in your business name, description, and posts.
2. **Consistent NAP (Name, Address, Phone)**:
   - Ensure your NAP details are the same across all platforms.
3. **Choose Local Categories**:

- Use industry-specific and location-relevant categories.

5. Collect and Manage Reviews

1. **Ask for Reviews**:
    - Encourage satisfied customers to leave Google reviews.
    - Share the direct review link with customers via email or SMS.
2. **Respond to Reviews**:
    - Thank positive reviewers.
    - Address negative reviews professionally to show you care about customer feedback.

6. Add Posts and Updates

Use Google Posts to share updates, offers, and events. These appear in your profile and attract customer attention.

1. **Types of Posts**:
    - **What's New**: Announcements or updates.
    - **Events**: Promotions, sales, or in-store activities.
    - **Offers**: Discounts or special deals.
    - **Products**: Showcase featured items.
2. **Post Tips**:
    - Use images and videos for better engagement.
    - Include a call-to-action (e.g., "Learn More," "Call Now").

7. Use GMB Features

1. **Add Products and Services**:
    - List your offerings, prices, and descriptions.
2. **Enable Messaging**:
    - Allow customers to message you directly through the profile.
3. **Set Up Bookings**:
    - Integrate booking tools to streamline appointment scheduling.
4. **Monitor Insights**:
    - Track profile performance, including views, searches, and customer actions.

8. Regularly Update and Monitor

1. **Keep Information Current**:
   - Update hours, contact details, and offerings as needed.
2. **Monitor Competitors**:
   - Review their profiles for inspiration and benchmarking.
3. **Respond Quickly to Customer Questions**:
   - Use the Q&A feature to answer FAQs.

Step 9: Integrate with Other Marketing Channels

- **Website**: Ensure your site matches the information on GMB.
- **Social Media**: Share GMB updates on platforms like Facebook and Instagram.
- **Local Listings**: Ensure your profile is consistent with other local directories.

Step 10: Avoid Common Pitfalls

1. **Avoid Keyword Stuffing**:
   - Do not overuse keywords; focus on natural language.
2. **Maintain Accurate Information**:
   - Incorrect or outdated info can frustrate customers.
3. **Comply with Guidelines**:
   - Follow Google's policies to avoid suspension.

Why Optimize Your Google Business Profile?

1. **Improved Local Search Visibility**:
   - Appear in the "Local Pack" and Google Maps searches.
2. **Better Customer Engagement**:
   - Increased calls, messages, and visits.
3. **Build Trust**:
   - A well-maintained profile signals professionalism.

OPTIMATE SOCIAL MEDIA PROFILES

Toprankedvideo.com

Call Us: 954-839-8684
Follow: @quickregisterseo

2. Optimize Your Social Media Profiles

Optimizing your social media accounts is essential for improving your online presence and supporting the ranking of your **Google My Business (GMB)** pages. Here's a detailed guide to help you get started and maximize your efforts:

1. Ensure NAP Consistency Across Platforms

- **NAP** stands for **Name, Address, and Phone number**, and it's crucial that this information is consistent across all your social media accounts and directories.
- **Why Consistency Matters**: Google values consistent information because it confirms the legitimacy and accuracy of your business. Inconsistent details can confuse search engines and customers, negatively impacting your rankings.
- **How to Check for Consistency**:
    1. Audit your current social media profiles.
    2. Cross-check your NAP details with what is listed on your GMB page.
    3. Update any discrepancies immediately.

2. Focus on High-Impact Social Media Platforms

- Most businesses are already active on major platforms like:
    - Facebook
    - Instagram
    - LinkedIn
    - Twitter (X)
- While these are essential, Google also values citations from smaller, niche platforms that may not be on your radar.

3. Explore Lesser-Known but Valuable Social Media Sites

- There are over **100 social media and directory sites** that you can leverage. Many of these are particularly valued for **SEO citations** and local rankings. Visit here to see a list.

    As a new client of Toprankedvideo.com we will create **100 additional social media accounts and fully optimize them for you.**

4. Optimize Each Social Media Profile

- Use **local keywords** strategically:
    - Include **keywords related to your services and location** in profile descriptions, bios, and about sections.
    - Example: Instead of "Professional Plumber," use **"Licensed Plumber in [City Name]."**
- Add a **call to action (CTA)**:
    - Examples: "Call us today for a free quote!" or "Visit us at [website link]."
- Use high-quality branding elements:
    - Upload a **professional profile picture** (e.g., your logo) and a visually appealing cover photo.
    - Ensure your **branding is consistent across platforms**.
- Update **categories and services:**
    - Many platforms allow you to choose business categories. Select the **most relevant ones.**
- Include **links to your website**, **GMB page**, and other profiles to interconnect your online presence.

5. Boost the Value of Your Citations

- Social media profiles act as **citations**—references to your business across the web.
- Each profile linking to your GMB page or website **reinforces the authority** and trustworthiness of your business in Google's eyes.
- To maximize this:
    - Add a **link to your website in every profile's bio** or website field.
    - Use **consistent branding** across all platforms.
    - **Share content** (even occasionally) to keep profiles active, as inactive profiles can lose authority over time.

6. Automate the Submission Process

- Submitting to over 100 sites can be tedious, but there are tools that streamline the

process:
- **BrightLocal**: Automates citation building and keeps track of your NAP consistency.
- **Moz Local**: Distributes your business data to key directories.
- **Yext**: Automates listings on hundreds of platforms but can be costly.
- **Ubersuggest** or **SEMrush**: Provide insights into which directories and citations might benefit your niche.

7. Monitor and Update Regularly

- Regularly review your social media profiles to ensure:
  - NAP consistency is maintained.
  - Any changes in your business (e.g., address, phone number) are updated.
  - Keywords and descriptions remain relevant to your business goals and local SEO strategies.
- Use tools like **Google Alerts** to monitor mentions of your business and stay on top of changes.

8. Measure the Impact

- Track how these optimizations influence your rankings and visibility:
  - Use **Google Analytics** to track traffic from social media sites.
  - Check your GMB insights to see if the number of views, calls, and website clicks increases.
  - Run periodic local SEO audits using tools like **Whitespark** or **SEMrush**.

VIDEO MARKETING

Toprankedvideo.com

Call Us: 954-839-8684
Follow: @quickregisterseo

3. Using Video Marketing to Increase Traffic Leads and Sales for Local Businesses

Video marketing is one of the **most effective ways to increase exposure for your local business.**

With **Google owning YouTube**—the **second-largest search engine after Google** itself—creating and optimizing video content can **improve your visibility in both Google search** results and **Google Video** rankings.

Here's a comprehensive guide to leveraging video marketing for your local business:

1. Why Video Marketing Matters for Local Businesses

- **Boost Engagement**: Videos capture attention and engage viewers more effectively than text or images alone.
- **SEO Advantages**: YouTube videos are often prominently featured in Google search results, giving you a dual opportunity to rank on both platforms.
- **Local Trust and Connection**: Videos build trust by allowing potential customers to see your face, hear your voice, and understand your business on a personal level.
- **Social Media Amplification**: Platforms like TikTok, Instagram, and Facebook prioritize video content, making it easier to reach your target audience.

2. Types of Videos to Create

- **Educational Videos**
    - **Answer common customer questions** or explain your services in a way that adds value to your community.
    - Example: A local plumber could create a video titled, *"How to Fix a Leaky Faucet in 5 Simple Steps."*
- **Top 10 Lists**
    - Highlight your expertise with **"Top 10" videos.**
    - Example: *"Top 10 Reasons to Visit [Your Town] This Weekend"* or *"Top 10 Benefits of Choosing [Your Service]."*
- **Customer Testimonials**

- **Ask satisfied customers to share their experiences on camera.** Video testimonials feel more authentic and compelling than text reviews.
- Example: A fitness trainer could feature a client talking about their success story. For example, we created a video using the testimonials from one of our clients and optimized for search
  - **Case Studies**
    - **Showcase your problem-solving skills** with **real-life examples** of how your services have helped customers.
    - Example: A digital marketer could create a video demonstrating how they increased a client's traffic by 50%.
  - **Interviews**
    - **Host interviews** with yourself or industry experts. **Zoom interviews work perfectly** for this, and they can be pre-recorded or streamed live.
    - Example: *"Behind the Scenes: How We Started [Your Business Name]"* or *"Ask an Expert: Tips for [Industry-Specific Problem]."*
  - **Live Events and Seminars**
    - **Record live events**, workshops, or webinars and run them as live or pre-recorded content to reach a wider audience.
    - Example: A local real estate agent could run a virtual seminar on *"How to Buy Your First Home."*
  - **Virtual Tours and Demonstrations**
    - Give viewers a **behind-the-scenes look at your business** or showcase your product in action.
    - Example: A restaurant could create a virtual tour of their kitchen and dining space.

---

3. Optimizing Your Videos for Search Engines

- **Use Local Keywords**:
  - **Incorporate your city, neighborhood, or service area in video** titles, descriptions, and tags.
  - Example: *"Best Italian Restaurant in [City Name]: A Virtual Tour"*.
- **Add a Call-to-Action (CTA)**:
  - **Direct viewers to your website**, GMB page, or social media profiles.
  - Example: *"Visit us at [website link] or call [phone number] for reservations!"*
- **Include NAP Details**:
  - Add your **Name, Address, and Phone number** in the video description to reinforce your local SEO.
- **Leverage YouTube Playlists**:
  - Group **similar videos into playlists** to keep viewers engaged and signal relevance to search engines.

4. Leverage Social Media Platforms
- **YouTube**:
  - As the most powerful video platform, **YouTube should be your primary focus**. Regularly upload and optimize videos for SEO.
- **TikTok**:
  - Create short, entertaining videos that showcase your personality or quick tips related to your business.
  - Example: *"3 Easy Fixes for Common Plumbing Problems"* (30 seconds).
- **Instagram**:
  - Use **Instagram Reels** and Stories to share short, engaging content.
  - Example: A bakery could post behind-the-scenes videos of cakes being decorated.
- **Facebook**:
  - or run them as Facebook Ads for local targeting.

5. Tips for High-Quality Video Content
- **Keep it Short and Engaging**:
  - Most videos should be under 2 minutes, especially on platforms like TikTok and Instagram.
- **Use Professional Tools**:
  - Invest in good lighting, clear audio, and stable video recording equipment.
- **Be Authentic**:
  - Audiences connect more with genuine content than overly polished, scripted videos.
- **Use Captions**:
  - Many people watch videos without sound, so include captions to increase accessibility.

6. Promote Your Videos Effectively
- **Cross-Promote**:
  - Share your videos across all platforms, including your website and email newsletters.
- **Run Ads**:
  - Use targeted advertising on YouTube, Facebook, and Instagram to reach local audiences.
- **Collaborate**:
  - Partner with other local businesses or influencers for joint video projects to expand your reach.
- **Engage Your Audience**:
  - Encourage likes, shares, and comments to boost your video's visibility.

7. Measure Your Success
- Use analytics tools to track:
    - Views, likes, and shares.
    - Website traffic from video links.
    - Engagement metrics like comments or questions.

Using Video as a Tool For Reputation Management Transforming Reviews into Video Content

Taking written reviews from platforms like Google My Business (GMB) and converting them into video content is an excellent way to amplify positive customer experiences.

Case Study: DPS Health and Wellness

For our client **DPS Health and Wellness**, we transformed their GMB reviews into engaging videos. Each video highlighted glowing customer feedback, showcasing the benefits of their services.

Results:

- **Search Domination**: When potential customers searched for "DPS Health and Wellness Reviews" on YouTube or Google, they were greeted with these positive review videos dominating the top search results.
- **Improved Trust**: Video testimonials feel more authentic and impactful than text alone, increasing viewer trust in the business.

Steps to Replicate:

1. **Collect Reviews**:
    - Identify the most compelling reviews from your GMB page or other review sites.
2. **Create Video Content**:
    - Use tools like Canva, Animoto, or Adobe Premiere to create visually appealing videos.
    - Include a voiceover or text overlay to narrate the review.
    - Incorporate background music and images of your business for added impact.
3. **Optimize for SEO**:
    - Use keywords like *"[Your Business Name] Reviews"* in the title, description, and tags.
    - Example: *"DPS Health and Wellness – Real Customer Reviews & Testimonials."*
4. **Upload and Promote**:
    - Share the videos on YouTube, your website, and across social media platforms.

dps health and wellness reviews

Number 1 in search!

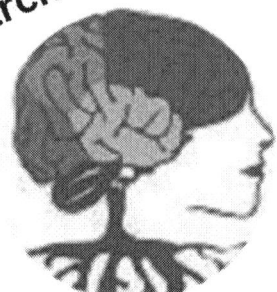

Highlighting Customer Success Stories

Beyond reviews, creating case study videos is another way to manage your reputation. Showcase real-life examples of how your business solved a problem or provided exceptional service.

Example:

A physical therapy clinic could record a video featuring a patient sharing their recovery journey. The client can explain how the clinic's care helped them return to their daily life, reinforcing the business's credibility.

Proactive Response to Negative Feedback

Even the best businesses receive occasional negative reviews. Video marketing can help you turn the narrative around by emphasizing your commitment to customer satisfaction.

Tactics:

- **Address Concerns Publicly:**
    - Create a video explaining how you've resolved an issue mentioned in a negative review, showing your dedication to improvement.
    - Example: *"How We're Improving Our Services Based on Your Feedback."*
- **Overwhelm Negativity with Positivity:**
    - Produce more positive review videos to drown out the impact of any negative content in search results.

Promoting Awards and Certifications

If your business has received accolades, certifications, or industry recognition, video marketing is the perfect medium to showcase these achievements.

Example:

A dentist could create a video titled, *"Award-Winning Dental Care in [City Name] – What Patients Are Saying"*, combining visuals of the award with customer testimonials.

Leveraging User-Generated Content

Encourage your happy customers to create video testimonials or record their experiences using your services. User-generated content (UGC) is perceived as more authentic and can significantly bolster your reputation.

Example:
A gym could invite members to share short videos of their fitness progress, tagging the business on social media.

Optimizing Videos for Reputation Management

To ensure your videos rank high in search results and overshadow any negative press or feedback:

- **Use Targeted Keywords:**
    - Focus on keywords like *"[Business Name] Reviewsm" "Top Rated [Industry] in [City]"*, or *"Customer Feedback for [Business Name]."*
- **Embed Videos on Your Website:**
    - Add your review and testimonial videos to relevant pages to reinforce credibility for visitors.
- **Build Playlists:**
    - On YouTube, organize positive review videos into playlists, such as *"Customer Success Stories"* or *"What People Are Saying About Us."*

Distributing Videos Across Multiple Platforms

- **YouTube:**
    - The primary platform for reputation management due to its visibility in Google search results.
- **Social Media:**
    - Share videos on Facebook, Instagram, and TikTok to engage your audience and encourage shares.
- **Email Campaigns:**
    - Include review videos in email newsletters to strengthen relationships with existing customers and attract new ones.

Monitoring Results

Track the performance of your reputation management videos by monitoring:

- **Search Rankings:**
    - Check if your videos appear in the top search results for queries like *"[Business Name] Reviews."*
- **Engagement Metrics:**
    - Monitor views, likes, shares, and comments to gauge effectiveness.
- **Customer Sentiment:**
    - Pay attention to new reviews or customer feedback mentioning your videos.

Final Thoughts

Video marketing is an indispensable tool for managing and enhancing your local business's reputation.

By **converting positive reviews into videos**, sharing customer success stories, and proactively addressing concerns, you can **control how your business is perceived online.**

When done strategically, **your videos will dominate search results**, build trust, and attract **more customers.**

CREATE A BUSINESS BLOG

Toprankedvideo.com

Call Us: 954-839-8684
Follow: @quickregisterseo

4. Creating Your Own Blog for Local Businesses

Starting a blog for your local business is a powerful way to connect with your community, build authority in your niche, and **improve your visibility online.**

A well-maintained blog allows you to **showcase your expertise, share updates**, and **provide valuable information** that resonates with your audience.

Whether you're a **personal injury attorney,** a home inspection service specializing in **mold testing,** a café owner, or a fitness trainer, creating content tailored to local interests—such as legal advice for accident victims, tips for preventing mold in your home, or community event roundups—can **set you apart as a trusted resource.**

From an SEO perspective, blogging is one of the **most effective ways to rank for local search** terms. By incorporating relevant keywords, such as *"top personal injury attorney in [Your City]"* or *"affordable mold testing in [Your Region],"* your blog posts can help your website appear in **search engine results** for **potential customers in your area.**

Additionally, blogging gives you the chance to link to your Google My Business page, social media profiles, and other pages on your website, which enhances your overall online presence.

Embedding videos into your blog posts further **amplifies these SEO benefits** by increasing dwell time—**how long visitors stay on your site**—and providing another opportunity to **rank in Google's video search results**.

Videos add an engaging, dynamic element to your blog. For example, a personal injury attorney could embed a video explaining the **steps to take immediately after an accident.**

While a home inspector might include a **walk through of a recent mold testing process** and the tools used.

Videos like these not only educate your audience but also **build trust by demonstrating expertise. Google prioritizes pages with multimedia content**, meaning embedding videos in your posts can boost search rankings significantly.

By **combining well-written blog posts with engaging videos,** you can maximize your impact, **attract more local customers**, and establish your business as a trusted leader in your community.

OPTIMIZE FOR VOICE SEARCH

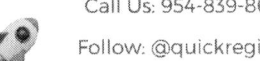

Call Us: 954-839-8684

Follow: @quickregisterseo

5. Optimizing for Voice Search

Voice search is rapidly **transforming how consumers find local businesses,** with the growing popularity of **voice-activated devices like smartphones, smart speakers**, and virtual assistants such as **Siri, Alexa, and Google Assistant.**

To tap into this trend, businesses must **optimize their online presence for voice search queries**, which tend to be more **conversational and question-based** than traditional typed searches.

For example, instead of searching **"mold testing near me,"** a voice search might be, *"Who offers affordable mold testing services in my area?"* Adjusting your content strategy to incorporate these **natural-language phrases** can help your business appear in **voice search results.**

Start by **ensuring your website content answers common questions your target audience might ask**. Creating a frequently asked questions **(FAQ) section** is a great way to include these **long-tail, conversational keywords.**

Additionally, **focusing on local SEO is crucial** since most voice searches have a local intent, such as finding a nearby service provider or business.

Make sure your Google My Business **(GMB) profile is complete, accurate,** and up to date, as virtual assistants often pull data directly from GMB listings.

Finally, ensure your website is **mobile-friendly** and loads quickly since most voice searches are conducted on mobile devices.

By adapting your content and SEO practices to align with voice search trends, you can **stay ahead of the competition** and capture the attention of this growing segment of search users.

6. Using Press Releases to Promote Local Businesses

Using press releases for local businesses Is an effective way to generate visibility and attract attention from both media outlets and local consumers.

Press releases can be used to **announce new products or services,** special events, community involvement, partnerships, or any notable milestones your business reaches.

By distributing your **press release to local news outlets**, industry publications, and online platforms, you increase your chances of being featured in stories that will reach a wider audience.

Press releases also offer SEO benefits, as they often include **back links to your website,** which can improve your search engine rankings.

When **optimized with relevant keywords and local details,** press releases not only boost your **business's credibility** but also help establish it as an active, engaged participant in the local community.

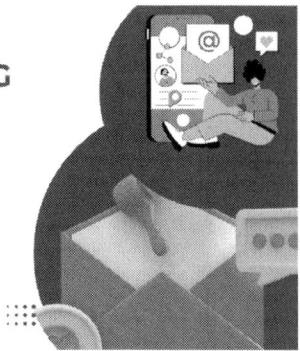

EMAIL MAKRETING FOR LOCAL BUSINESSES

Toprankedvideo.com

Call Us: 954-839-8684

Follow: @quickregisterseo

7. Using Email Marketing Effectively

Here are 10 ways email marketing can be used for local businesses:

- **Promote Special Offers and Discounts**: Send exclusive offers to your local subscribers, such as limited-time discounts, BOGO deals, or seasonal promotions.

- **Announce New Products or Services**: Inform your local audience about new offerings or updates to existing products and services, keeping them engaged.

- **Send Event Invitations**: Promote local events, grand openings, or workshops and encourage customers to attend.

- **Seasonal Reminders**: Send timely reminders for services related to the seasons, such as HVAC check-ups, mold testing, or lawn care.

- **Build Customer Loyalty**: Offer loyalty rewards or a VIP program to your email subscribers, encouraging repeat business.

- **Share Customer Testimonials and Reviews**: Include positive feedback from local customers to build trust and credibility.

- **Provide Educational Content**: Share useful tips, how-to guides, or blog posts that help your customers solve problems or learn something new.

- **Request Feedback and Reviews**: Ask customers for feedback after a service and encourage them to leave reviews on your Google My Business or Yelp page.

- **Send Birthday or Anniversary Greetings**: Personalize emails with special offers or messages for customer birthdays or anniversaries.
- **Highlight Local Community Involvement**: Showcase your business's participation in local events, charity work, or collaborations with other community businesses.

SMS MARKETING FOR LOCAL BUSINESSES

Toprankedvideo.com

Call Us: 954-839-8684

Follow: @quickregisterseo

8. Use SMS Marketing

Promote Time-Sensitive Offers: Send exclusive, limited-time promotions or discounts to create urgency and drive immediate action.

- **Event Announcements**: Inform customers about upcoming local events, sales, or new product launches.

- **Appointment Reminders**: Send reminders to customers about upcoming appointments, bookings, or reservations.

- **Exclusive Local Discounts**: Offer special deals to customers in specific locations to encourage foot traffic to your store or business.

- **Confirm Orders or Bookings**: Use SMS to confirm orders, reservations, or service appointments, ensuring a smooth customer experience.

- **High Engagement Rate**: Take advantage of SMS's high open rate, with most messages being read within minutes.

- **Targeted Location-Based Messaging**: Segment your customer list based on location and send tailored messages to nearby customers.

- **Increase Sales and Traffic**: Drive foot traffic and boost sales with personalized, direct communication via SMS.

PAID ADS FOR LOCAL BUSINESSES

Toprankedvideo.com

Call Us: 954-839-8684

Follow: @quickregisterseo

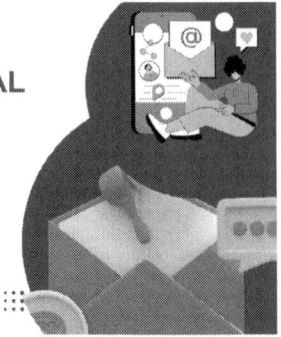

8. Use Paid Advertising with Local Targeting

Leverage Google Ads with Location Targeting: Use Google Ads to target specific geographic areas by setting location parameters. This ensures your ads are shown to potential customers near your business.

- **Utilize Facebook and Instagram Ads**: Both platforms allow businesses to target local audiences based on location, interests, behaviors, and more, making them ideal for localized promotions.

- **Geo-Fencing with Mobile Ads**: Use geo-fencing technology to deliver ads to customers within a defined geographic area, such as near your store or event, encouraging immediate visits or actions.

- **Promote Local Offers or Discounts**: Use paid ads to showcase special offers or events tailored to local customers, increasing the likelihood of attracting foot traffic.

- **Target Specific Demographics**: Narrow your audience based on local demographics, such as age, gender, or income level, to reach the most relevant local prospects.

- **Use Google My Business for Local Search Ads**: Pair Google Ads with your Google My Business listing to show ads in local search results, increasing visibility when users search for local services.

- **Take Advantage of Yelp Ads**: Advertise your business on Yelp to reach local customers actively searching for services like yours in your area.

- **Leverage YouTube Ads for Local Exposure**: Use YouTube's geo-targeting to deliver video ads to users in specific locations, showcasing your local expertise and services.

- **Optimize Ads for Mobile Devices**: Since many local searches happen on mobile devices, ensure your paid ads are optimized for mobile viewing and easy interaction.

- **Monitor and Adjust Your Budget**: Track the performance of your ads within local areas and adjust your budget to ensure the best ROI, focusing more on high-performing locations.

Promoting your YouTube videos can be an effective way to build your brand. At Toprankedvideo.com we can manage and create YouTube video campaigns for you.

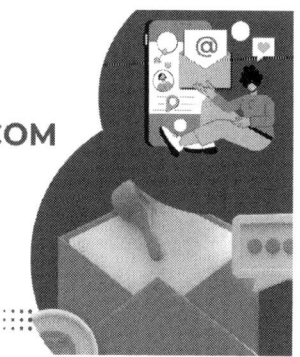

BUY LOCAL SEO TRAFFIC
REALPPVTRAFFIC.COM

Toprankedvideo.com

Call Us: 954-839-8684
Follow: @quickregisterseo

9. Buy SEO Traffic From Realppvtraffic SEO Traffic

Traffic is a key factor in determining your website's ranking in local search results. Google views high-quality, consistent traffic as an indicator that **your website is valuable and relevant to users,** which can directly influence your search engine rankings.

The **more visitors your site receives**—especially from local searches—the more likely Google is to perceive your business as a **trusted, authoritative source in your industry.**

To boost traffic, consider using targeted SEO services like Realppvtraffic.com which specializes in **driving organic, high-converting traffic tailored to your specific location and niche.**

By **attracting local visitors who are actively searching for your products or services,** you not only enhance your online presence but also improve your chances of ranking higher in local search results, ultimately driving **more potential customers to your site.**

Keep in mind all the methods work together to **give you momentum.**

A dead site generally does not get found in Google.

GET LISTED IN LOCAL DIRECTORIES SPECIFICALLY FOR LOCAL BUSINESSES

Toprankedvideo.com

Call Us: 954-839-8684

Follow: @quickregisterseo

10. Get Listed in Local Directories

Getting your business listed in **local directories like Yelp, Angie's List,** and others is a crucial step in improving your online visibility and local search rankings.

These platforms provide an easy way for potential customers to discover your business while also offering valuable citations for SEO.

By ensuring that your **business information is accurate and up-to-date across various directories,** you not only improve your chances of being found by local consumers but also **enhance your reputation** through customer reviews and engagement.

Listing your business in local directories is a simple yet effective strategy for boosting both your online presence and local credibility.

Increase Online Visibility: Listing your business in local directories like Yelp, Angie's List, and Yellow Pages helps improve visibility and makes it easier for potential customers to find your business online.

- **Enhance Local SEO**: Local directory listings act as "citations" that signal to search engines that your business is relevant to a specific geographic area, which can improve your local search rankings.

- **Provide Accurate Business Information**: Ensure your business name, address, phone number (NAP), website, and hours of operation are accurate and consistent across all listings, as this improves SEO and customer trust.

- **Improve Reputation Management**: These directories often allow customers to leave reviews. Positive reviews can enhance your credibility, while addressing negative reviews demonstrates customer service and responsiveness.

- **Attract More Local Customers**: Local directories are a go-to resource for people searching for businesses in their area. Being listed increases your chances of being found by local customers looking for services like yours.

- **Stand Out in Industry-Specific Directories**: In addition to general directories, get listed in industry-specific directories (e.g., health, home services, restaurants) to target a more relevant audience and build specialized credibility.

- **Add Photos and Videos**: Many local directories allow businesses to add images or videos. Use this to showcase your products, services, or customer testimonials, giving potential clients a visual reason to contact you.

- **Optimize Your Profile**: Complete your directory profiles with detailed descriptions of your services, special offers, or expertise. This provides customers with valuable information and increases the likelihood of them reaching out.

- **Link Back to Your Website**: Many local directories allow businesses to include a link to their website, which drives traffic and boosts your website's authority.

- **Stay Active and Engage with Customers**: Respond to reviews and keep your directory profiles up to date. Active engagement shows that you care about customer feedback and enhances your online reputation.

Partner with Local Organizations: Build relationships with local businesses, nonprofits, and community organizations. Consider **sponsoring local events**, writing guest blog posts for local websites, or partnering on community projects. These links will not only **drive traffic** but also **boost your local authority in search engines**.

ON PAGE SEO

OPTIMIZE WITH ON PAGE LOCAL SEO

Toprankedvideo.com

Call Us: 954-839-8684

Follow: @quickregisterseo

11. Use On-Page SEO to Optimize Your Website for Local Searches

On-page SEO is a critical technique for improving your website's search rankings, especially for local searches. Here are some key tactics:

- **Local Keyword Optimization**: Include keywords that are specific to your services and location. For example, a plumber in Chicago might target "plumbing services in Chicago" or "**emergency plumber in Chicago**." These should appear in your page titles, headings, meta descriptions, and throughout the content.
- **Location Pages**: If you serve multiple locations, **create a dedicated page for each area you serve**. These pages should be optimized with the relevant city or **neighborhood names**.
- **Schema Markup**: Use **Local Business Schema** markup to help search engines understand more about your business (name, address, phone number, reviews, etc.). This can **improve your visibility in local searches** and potentially lead to rich snippets in search results.
- **Mobile Optimization**: With the rise of mobile searches, **ensuring your website is mobile-friendly is crucial**. Google prioritizes mobile-first indexing, so if your website isn't mobile-optimized, your rankings will suffer.

Effective on-page SEO not only helps search engines understand your website better but also ensures your **site is user-friendly, ultimately improving conversion rates and sales.**

Create Location-Specific Content

Creating location-specific content is an effective way to **capture local traffic** and improve your local SEO rankings. Focus on producing blog posts, videos, or landing pages that are tailored to the needs and interests of your local audience. Here are some ideas:

- **Local Guides**: Write blog posts or create videos about local events, guides to your city, or "best-of" lists. For example, a local gym could create a blog post or video about "The Top 5 Hiking Trails in [City Name]" or a hair salon might create a guide to the best wedding venues in the area.
- **Local News and Events**: Stay involved in your community and share news, updates, and events on your website and social media. This not only helps with SEO by including local keywords, but it also demonstrates your business's connection to the community.
- **Local Case Studies and Testimonials**: Share success stories and testimonials from local customers. Creating a dedicated case study page or video series with local customer experiences helps build credibility and trust while boosting SEO.

CROSS PROMOTE WITH LOCAL INFLUENCERS

Toprankedvideo.com

Call Us: 954-839-8684

Follow: @quickregisterseo

12. Cross Promote With Local Influencers

Are there other **local businesses that do not compete but complement your business**. You can talk about each other on each others social media pages. You **can interview each other. Do events together.** You can post these events on your websites, blogs and social media pages.

13. Classified Ads

Yes, Craigslist is still around and you can **post ads on Craigslist.** There is also a service that will **submit ads for you all year long called Classifiedsubmissions.com.** This is a very **low cost way to get traffic** to your website and social media pages and as we said before traffic itself can help you **get noticed in Google**.

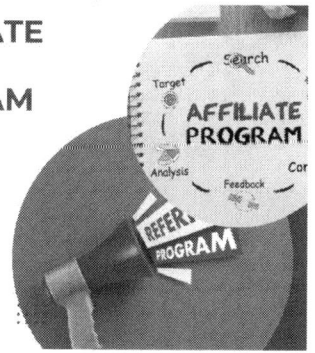

14. Create A Referral (Affiliate Program)

Amazon started this and **offering cash or other incentives for people to refer you** can be very profitable. Essentially people do the advertising for you and you only pay them when they sell something.

There are various types of **software that can be installed on your website** to track sales or you can even offer special discounts codes to specific affiliates or influencers to track affiliate sales.

We run 4 different affiliate programs and we have made $100,000's of dollars with this method.

As you can see there are **almost endless ways to promote your local business.** The problem is having the **time and expertise to implement these strategies**.

This is why it can be wise to **delegate this work to the experts.**

Please visit Toprankedvideo.com local marketing solutions.. We can even **create custom tailored promotions** to specifically for your business.

You can also **contact us directly at (954) 839-8684**. We can then look at your business and come up with solutions that fit your specific needs.

We can **only accept a limited number of clients since we always over deliver**. We are looking for clients who are committed to **dominating their niche for the long term.**

Wishing You Much Success With Your Local Business,

Matthew May
Toprankedvideo.com

DONE FOR YOU MARKETING SERVICES FOR LOCAL BUSINESSES

Toprankedvideo.com

Call Us: 954-839-8684

Follow: @quickregisterseo

Are you an **affiliate marketer**? You can now **re-brand this valuable ebook** with your own **affiliate links** to **3 free to join affiliate programs**. Give this book away to local businesses and if they order any of our services you get paid **recurring affiliate commissions**.

Learn more about our affiliate program here.

Re-brand this ebook with here your own affiliate links in just seconds with our online re-brander.

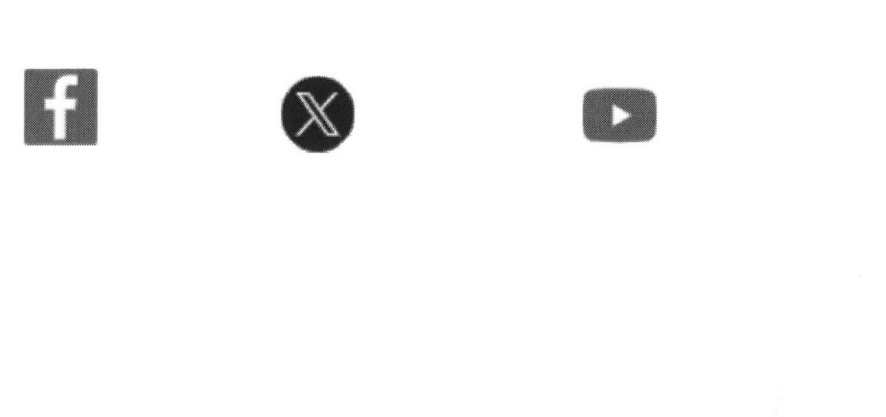

Printed in Dunstable, United Kingdom